Alternative
ENERGY

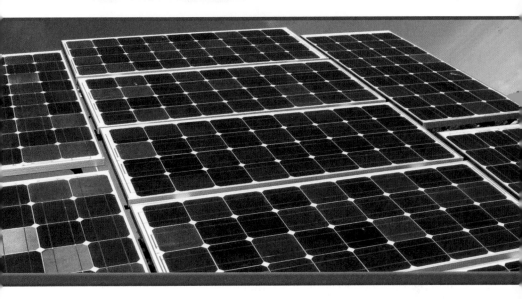

Rob Waring, *Series Editor*

HEINLE
CENGAGE Learning

Australia • Brazil • Japan • Korea • Mexico • Singapore • Spain • United Kingdom • United States

Words to Know

This story is set in the United States. It takes place just south of Boulder, Colorado.

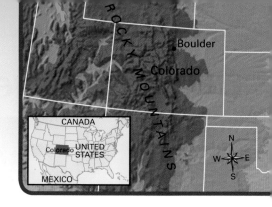

 A **Fossil Fuels.** Read the paragraph. Then write the correct underlined word or phrase next to each definition.

The world is currently facing a growing crisis over finding sustainable sources of energy. Many countries presently depend upon fossil fuels for energy, which is having a negative effect on global warming. In the U.S., the burning of fossil fuels, such as the gasoline used in most cars, is responsible for more than 90 percent of the greenhouse gases that are contributing to climate problems. The issue has become so great that the search for viable alternatives to fossil fuels has now become urgent.

1. practical; realistic: _____
2. a liquid form of fuel often used in engines: _____
3. able to continue or lasting for a long time: _____
4. materials that release heat when burned to provide energy: _____
5. atmospheric gases that reduce Earth's loss of heat into space: _____
6. an increase in world temperatures caused by gases that stop heat from escaping into space: _____

The Fossil Fuels Coal and Oil

pieces of coal

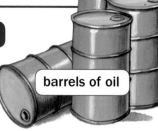
barrels of oil

Alternative Energy. Read the paragraph. Then match each word or phrase with the correct definition.

At the National Renewable Energy Laboratory, scientists are working to find energy resources that are efficient and easily replaced. Their goal is to find cost-effective alternatives to fossil fuels, such as using wind turbines to collect the power of the wind, or solar cells to harness the energy of the sun. They're even researching the use of grains such as corn to produce ethanol fuel, which can be used to power vehicles.

1. renewable _____	**a.** a device that converts the power of the sun into electrical energy
2. cost-effective _____	**b.** producing the best results for the amount of money spent
3. wind turbine _____	**c.** a liquid source of energy that can be used as an alternative to gasoline
4. solar cell _____	**d.** able to be used again or continued
5. harness _____	**e.** capture the power of something
6. ethanol _____	**f.** a machine that produces electricity using blades turned by wind

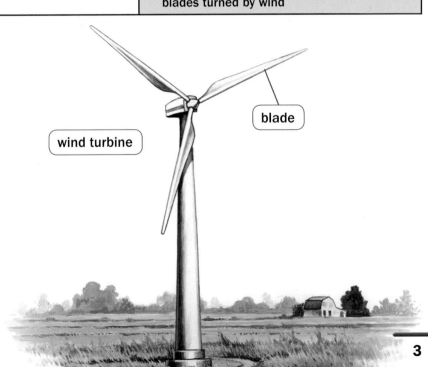

blade

wind turbine

The world seems to have an **insatiable**[1] appetite for oil, electricity, and natural gas; however, fossil fuels may not have much of a future. Present resources of these natural fuels are in shorter and shorter supply. In addition, their use has been proven to be a contributing factor in global warming, and partly responsible for the current environmental crises on Earth. The world is now faced with a challenging problem: how to find cost-effective and sustainable alternatives to fossil fuels. Therefore, scientists are looking to the wind, the sun, and agricultural products to power our future.

Sandy Butterfield of the National Wind Technology Center near Boulder, Colorado, is absolutely convinced that harnessing the power of the wind could make a difference for the world's future. He points out that even with winds of just 25 kilometers* an hour, wind turbines start moving and have the capacity to create energy. However, when the wind blows fiercely, production increases and it seems that wind power could actually compete with fossil fuels as a viable, realistic source of energy. "I think the past **perception**[2] was that wind energy was nice," he says, "but not a real solution. That perception is changing. I see wind energy getting more and more competitive." The wind is definitely an important source of sustainable energy, however it isn't the only available option.

---

[1]**insatiable:** not able to get enough of something; never satisfied
[2]**perception:** view; opinion
*See page 24 for a metric conversion chart.

 CD 3, Track 03

Skim for Gist

Read through the entire book quickly to answer the questions.

1. What is the book basically about?

2. What are two main points regarding the three energy sources described: the wind, the sun, and agricultural products?

Solar cells cover
an urban rooftop.

At the National Renewable Energy Laboratory (NREL) in Golden, Colorado, discovering alternative power sources that are competitive with fossil fuels has been a mission of scientists since the U.S. energy crisis of the 1970s. The importance of their work has recently grown as the need to find alternative energy sources has increased. This need for alternative renewable fuels is likely a direct result of the increased evidence regarding global warming, and an increased need to decrease the amount of greenhouse gases released into Earth's atmosphere.

The NREL's centers for science and technology support the research and development efforts of the U.S. Department of Energy. At the laboratories, scientists are often able to create alternative sources of energy that are far more efficient than those currently available to the public, including solar cells. Scientists and researchers at the center believe that the market for this technology is about to increase significantly. Their research indicates that people are ready to use solar power as an alternative to fossil fuels.

John Brenner, a scientist at the lab, reports: "Recent **polls**[3] have shown that about 75 percent of the population would favor the use of solar power, clean power, and would like to see more of it happening." With rising fuel prices, energy shortages, and environmental concerns, there has been an increasing interest in solar power technology. It has recently come to be an important item on many people's agendas and a main feature at conferences and meetings convening around the world.

---

[3]**poll:** a survey of opinion among people

However, when it comes to solar power, there seems to be a difference between what people say about having the option and what they actually do with it. Solar power has been around for centuries, but the reality is that people are still not using solar power in large amounts, even though in many instances it provides a viable and much cleaner alternative to fossil fuels. The 'solar revolution' that seemed to be inevitable 10 or 15 years ago simply hasn't been fully realized, especially in the U.S. It appears that while the public says they like the idea of using solar power, for many, incorporating it into their daily lives seems to be something that is reserved for the future, not now. Despite the large number of known benefits of solar power, in the past most people simply haven't welcomed its use in their homes as a primary or even supplementary energy source.

Not only is solar power clean compared to fossil fuels, but it can also make economic sense for consumers. **Larry Kazmerski**,[4] of the National Center for **Photovoltaics**[5] talks about people's attitudes toward solar power. "Sometimes, you know, you worry that they think that this is only a **fringe**[6] [movement], but it's not," he observes. "Photovoltaic, solar electricity, is becoming a technology that is becoming cost-effective for us as consumers in the United States."

---

[4]**Larry Kazmerski:** [kæzmɜrski]
[5]**photovoltaics:** the process of converting light into electricity using solar cells
[6]**fringe:** not commonly believed or practiced; extreme

In many people's opinion, it often takes a crisis for things to change. Historic events in the U.S., such as widespread power loss in the state of California at one point in recent history, have induced people to seriously consider the use of solar power. Kazmerski comments on the situation and its relevance to the search for alternative energy. "When your electricity doesn't come on in California," he laughs, "you start looking [for alternative fuels] very, very quickly!"

Luckily for some, using solar panels on the top of their houses to harness the power of the sun is becoming a viable alternative to the high costs of fossil fuels—especially in sunny climates like parts of California. Nowadays, home use of solar power is becoming more than just an abstract idea for more and more people. In fact, there are some 'adventurous' homeowners who have actually converted their homes entirely to solar energy, relying solely on solar power for their electricity.

Fact or Opinion?

Look at the following statements. Write 'F' for those that are factual, or 'O' for those that are an opinion.

1. Solar power isn't new. _____

2. Solar technology is a fringe activity. _____

3. It takes a crisis for things to change. _____

4. For more and more people, the use of solar power is becoming more than just an abstract idea. _____

A solar concentrator focuses the sun's rays into a narrow beam that turns an engine and provides electricity.

One homeowner using solar power exclusively is Jonathon Sawyer. When the solar electric system was first installed in his house in 1995, it was believed to be the largest residential solar system in the United States. This is likely due to the fact that solar power had not been widely promoted at the time. While that was years ago, the system is still so efficient that Sawyer actually sells electricity back to his local power company. Sawyer made the switch because he believes that changes on a larger, global scale can only occur when they begin on an individual level. He talks about his feelings on the subject: "I feel good because I've always been committed about the environment and doing something, and we have to start as individuals to do things."

Unfortunately, the reality of the situation is that individuals are only capable of doing so much. Researchers claim that for renewable energy to truly make a difference, it must be used on a large scale. A system called a 'solar concentrator' is often needed to produce solar power in larger amounts, but it's an option that can cause concerns due to its size. As he walks near one of the huge constructions, a reporter explains what the machine is and how it works. "This a solar concentrator," he begins gesturing to the huge mirrored structure. "The mirrors focus the sun's **rays**[7] into a narrow **beam,**[8] which turns an engine and provides electricity." Surprisingly, the man barely reaches the top of the concentrator's base. "Tough to get in the backyard? Sure," he jokes before adding, "but [a] power company could probably find a place for it."

---

[7]**ray:** a line of light, energy, or heat
[8]**beam:** a concentrated line of light

There are a number of factors preventing the full implementation of plans using alternative fuel sources, and several reasons why the change is occurring so slowly. One of the main factors is that the U.S. and other countries have often lacked a great sense of urgency to find energy alternatives. For decades, gasoline prices in these countries had been kept low due to government subsidies. Old habits persisted and people continued driving their large cars, usually alone.

Nowadays, though, gasoline costs are higher, and at times, price changes can affect people's work and personal lives. It is an economic situation that has enhanced the need to search for something else to fuel all those vehicles. This search has led scientists and researchers to find more unconventional fuel sources, including those created as **by-products**[9] of other processes.

In the U.S., a wealth of corn has led researchers to investigate its use as a potential alternative vehicle fuel source. Alternative fuel researcher John Sheehan explains how corn can be used to create ethanol. "What's in there now," he explains, pointing to a large machine, "is material that looks like straw. It's actually the material that farmers leave sitting on the ground after they go through and they harvest corn. We're trying to get farmers to collect this material so that we can run it through a conversion technology to make new liquid fuels."

---

[9]**by-product:** a secondary product deriving from a manufacturing process

An energy researcher shows an example of the kinds of materials that can be turned into fuel.

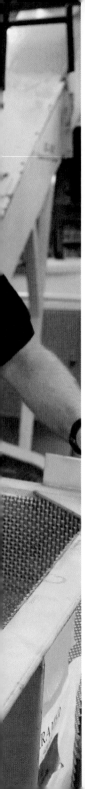

Since the global energy crisis of the 1970s, many farmers have been turning food into fuel by using grains like corn to create ethanol. But recently, some of the emphasis on making fuel has been moving away from the grain itself, to the **stalks**[10] and **stubble**[11] left on the ground after the harvest. Sheehan explains as he displays a number of packets containing grain stalks and stubble, "The **cellulose**[12] that's in here—that actually is made up of sugars—is something that they can turn into ethanol in the same way that they're currently taking the corn grain and having it turned into fuel-grade ethanol."

The National Renewable Energy Laboratory even has a manufacturing area that is capable of converting seemingly useless by-products left after the harvest— and just about anything else—into fuel. During a tour of the NREL facilities, Sheehan explains the various products that can be converted to replace fossil fuels. As he pauses in front of a row of boxes filled with various substances, he explains. "Some of these, like this for example," he says as he picks up a handful of a dry, brown substance, "is wood material." In fact, at the NREL they are researching the capacity to use trees, grasses, agricultural crops, or other biological materials as fuel, including simple wood chips.

---

[10] **stalk:** a stem of a plant
[11] **stubble:** the short pieces of grain (corn, wheat, etc.) in a field after the grain has been cut
[12] **cellulose:** a basic substance in nearly all plant cells

Proving that renewable energy technology is actually viable remains a struggle, at least in the U.S. Wind turbines, which were **pioneered**[13] in the U.S., are now being used by several countries in Europe to supply meaningful amounts of power, while their use in the U.S. remains relatively low. The main problem seems to be that, while fossil fuels may be unsustainable, they have remained relatively inexpensive. The U.S., for example, has traditionally had lower fuel prices than most of Europe, a situation that has lowered the immediate demand for alternate fuels.

Lower pricing of fossil fuels has also made it harder to convince people that these fuel supplies won't last forever. In this situation, economics has regularly beaten sustainability, and people have been inclined to take a short-term view since they have had little incentive to change. As Sandy Butterfield states in an earlier interview, "The cost of energy in the United States is so low compared to Europe, that our industry has had a harder time competing with fossil fuels."

Since that time, the cost of fuel has increased significantly in some countries, and while it has caused hardship, the cost increases have certain benefits. With this increase, the urgency to find reliable alternatives to fossil fuels will also likely increase. Hopefully, this will result in a subsequent increase in the funds available for alternative fuel research, and greater desire to implement alternative fuel programs. These changes may help fuel the demand for wind, solar, and other energy sources. The time for alternative energy may have arrived, and for those who use it, the future may be now.

---

[13]**pioneer:** be the first to develop and try

After You Read

1. What are agricultural products given as an example of on page 4?
   A. the world's insatiable appetite
   B. fossil fuels
   C. the present environmental crisis
   D. possible sources of energy

2. What does Sandy Butterfield claim on page 4?
   A. His organization deserves a government subsidy.
   B. The idea of using the power of the wind is still an abstract one.
   C. Fossil fuels can't create as much energy as wind turbines.
   D. Wind turbines are a competitive source of sustainable energy.

3. According to the writer, the desire to reduce the rate at which greenhouse gases are released is a result of:
   A. allowing us to use alternative energies
   B. concerns about the rate of global warming
   C. supporting the development efforts of scientists
   D. increasing the need for new sources of energies

4. What is the purpose of John Brenner's statement on page 7?
   A. to contrast alternative energies with fossil fuels
   B. to explain the need for meetings about solar energy
   C. to show that people's interest in using solar power is growing
   D. to place energy concerns at the top of the hierarchy of needs

5. What is the meaning of the word 'supplementary' on page 8?
   A. intrinsic
   B. secondary
   C. nuclear
   D. authentic

6. The public is not yet incorporating the technology of solar energy _____ their lives.
   A. within
   B. alongside
   C. by
   D. into

7. What opinion does Larry Kazmerski express on page 10?
   A. Sometimes it takes a crisis to induce change.
   B. Solar power is still too costly for consumers.
   C. U.S. citizens should all install solar panels.
   D. Scientists are worried about fringe movements.

8. An appropriate heading for paragraph 1 on page 13 is:
   A. Homeowner Buys Electricity from Government
   B. Individual Actions Help the Environment
   C. Risky Solar Power Harms the Adventurous
   D. Taxes Levied on Homes with Solar Panels

9. Which word on page 14 can be replaced by 'application?'
   A. implementation
   B. alternatives
   C. subsidies
   D. unconventional

10. What is being used more often to make ethanol?
    A. straw
    B. grains
    C. stalks
    D. stubble

11. In paragraph 1 on page 17, 'here' is referring to:
    A. farms
    B. the ground
    C. stalks and stubble
    D. the National Renewable Energy Laboratory

12. What conclusion does the writer NOT reach about the U.S.?
    A. The U.S. is creating technology for renewable energies.
    B. Fossil fuels have dominated the energy market in the U.S.
    C. Americans don't want to pay high prices for energy.
    D. There is no incentive for Americans to change their energy sources.

Energy News

A Major New Energy Source?

In the continuing search for sustainable sources to meet the world's growing demand for energy, scientists have taken a second look at a group of substances discovered by Sir Humphrey Davy in 1810. These materials are called 'calthrates' and they look a lot like ice.

THE FORMATION OF CALTHRATES

Calthrates are formed when two specific types of molecules combine. A molecule is the smallest piece of matter that has distinct chemical and physical properties. For example, air, water, and alcohol can all exist as molecules. Calthrates occur when a water molecule forms a cage-like structure around a smaller molecule and combines itself with this 'guest' molecule. Two of the most common guest molecules that combine with water in this way are the natural gas molecules methane and propane. Their formation involves water coming in contact with natural gas in a cool setting under high pressure. Therefore, large amounts of calthrates occur naturally at the bottom of the ocean, particularly in the polar regions, and even in some lakes in central Asia.

THE IMPORTANCE OF CALTHRATES

Because of the current energy crisis, scientists in many different countries are looking for ways to supplement existing fossil fuel sources. Some researchers believe that calthrates could supply more than twice the energy of all currently available fossil fuels combined. In the year 2000, the United States Senate authorized almost $50 million through the Methane Hydrate Research and Development Act so that the U.S. Department of Energy could begin an in-depth study of the energy

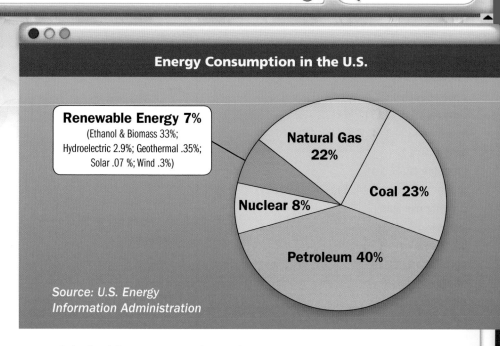

Energy Consumption in the U.S.

Renewable Energy 7%
(Ethanol & Biomass 33%;
Hydroelectric 2.9%; Geothermal .35%;
Solar .07 %; Wind .3%)

Natural Gas 22%

Coal 23%

Nuclear 8%

Petroleum 40%

*Source: U.S. Energy
Information Administration*

potential of calthrates. Since then, China and Japan, among others, have begun exploration projects in the waters surrounding their coastlines.

THE TROUBLE WITH CALTHRATES

Although calthrates offer a potentially plentiful supply of clean energy, there are two major problems. The first is that when the gases released from calthrates are burned, they contribute to global warming just like other fossil fuels. In fact, large amounts of harmful gases are released naturally when unstable underwater accumulations of calthrates break up and slide across the ocean floor, which could cause further problems for the environment. The second problem is that the technology involved in processing calthrates has proven to be too complicated and expensive to be considered a viable solution to our energy problems. However, researchers continue to explore new ways to safely release the energy of calthrates and to provide a solution to the world's energy shortage.

CD 3, Track 04

Word Count: 395
Time: _____

Vocabulary List

beam (12, 13)
by-product (14, 17)
cellulose (17)
cost-effective (3, 4, 8)
ethanol (3, 14, 17)
fossil fuel (2, 3, 4, 7, 8, 10, 17, 18)
fringe (8, 11)
gasoline (2, 3, 14)
global warming (2, 4, 7)
greenhouse gas (2, 7)
harness (3, 4, 10)
insatiable (4)
perception (4)
photovoltaic (8)
pioneer (18)
poll (7)
ray (12, 13)
renewable (3, 7, 13, 17, 18)
solar cell (3, 6, 7, 8)
stalk (17)
stubble (17)
sustainable (2, 4, 18)
viable (2, 4, 8, 18)
wind turbine (3, 4, 10, 18)

Metric Conversion Chart

Area
1 hectare = 2.471 acres

Length
1 centimeter = .394 inches
1 meter = 1.094 yards
1 kilometer = .621 miles

Temperature
0° Celsius = 32° Fahrenheit

Volume
1 liter = 1.057 quarts

Weight
1 gram = .035 ounces
1 kilogram = 2.2 pounds